THE COMPREHENSIVE DECOUPAGE FOR BEGINNERS GUIDE

INTRODUCTION

Cutting out photos, pasting them on anything, and then covering the entire piece with layers of varnish is simply known as découpage. The final product could pass for professionally painted if it is that gorgeous.

You can découpage just about anything around the house, and it's a great way to refurbish or lighten furniture that is starting to appear a little old and worn. Additionally, it can be used to create decorations for certain occasions, such as Christmas when making tree ornaments or Easter when decorating eggs with patterns and designs.

Decoupage is an enjoyable, tranquil, and calming activity that may be enjoyed by people of all ages and ability levels.

Therefore, paint household goods a new color or create

something eye-catching for your home. Here is a rundown of the tools you'll need and all the details you need to grasp about découpage.

Chapter 1

What is découpage?

Word découpage derives from the French verb découper, whose meaning is "to cut off." The découpage method may be used to personalize almost any item in your home, and the coolest part is that the designs can be as simple or complex as you like.

The beautiful thing about this hobby is that you undoubtedly already have a lot of the supplies at home, so you is means you can start working on simple projects right away! You can buy a wide variety of découpage-specific supplies. Simple materials and tools like scissors, a crafts knife, wrapping paper, magazines, and paper towels are required.

To get started, you only will require a few basic supplies and tools.

Chapter 2

What can you adorn with decoupage?

Almost anything may be decorated with decoupage using images. Vases, pots, and boxes, as well as bowls, trays, and plates, are popular objects.

- Lamps and lamp shades

- Furniture, frames, and mirrors

These could be items you already own but want to personalize or ones you bought solely for décor, like simple wooden boxes and frames.

Chapter 3

What are the best découpage papers?

Any type of paper may be used for découpage, which is one of its best features; the trick is to choose themes and patterns you enjoy and wish to incorporate into your art. Starting with papers you probablly already own or buying specific découpage papers are both options. They are available as cut-out drawings, thicker découpage paper, cut-out tissue paper, napkins, and even books whose pages may be pulled out and chopped up.

Before selecting a certain type of paper for your découpage project, consider the following information about each one.

Napkins with decoupage

Since napkins have more layers than tissues but are a little thicker, it is easier to cut out patterns from them when using them as decoupage materials. Although you can buy decoupage napkins, you may découpage on any napkin.

Tissue paper for decoupage

The designs on découpage tissue paper are very diverse, ranging from floral prints to vintage designs. The tissue paper is often two or three layers thick, even if the printed picture is just on the top layer. Because tissues are so thin, they are typically utilized to cover a surface by tearing up little segments and piecing them together to avoid creasing your pattern.

Rice paper decoupage

As soon as you begin to look at some decoupage sheets, you'll obviosly notice that they are made of rice paper. Because they are more fragile to use, these work well for découpage on glass. It's best to try them once you've finished some few decoupage projects and developed confidence.

Découpage paper Because it is thicker than découpage tissue paper and usually comes in large sizes, you may use it to cover an entire area without having to cut it into little pieces.

packaging paper

One of the most popular types of paper and a fantastic way to make crafts more ecologically friendly is to save and reuse the gift wrap from gifts you receive. It's fun to go wrapping paper shopping as well. Keep an eye out for patterns because Paperchase and other merchants frequently alter their stock of wrapping paper.

Magazines/catalogues

A fantastic way to utilize those outdated Prima copies! is by Cutting letters and sentences from catalogs and magazines is a terrific way to integrate messaging in your project.

Decorative books

Books with pages of découpage sheets and motifs featuring a certain theme, such as people or animals, are available for purchase. Because there are so many alternatives, you may be very inventive when combining various materials and cutouts, making these books an amazing value.

Greeting cards

Another fantastic way to craft in a sustainable manner. Never throw away a card without first taking out any pictures or patterns since they can be utilized in découpage. A 3D decoupage effect is an alternative to standard découpage and is especially effective on greeting cards. It includes overlaying cut-out motifs with 3D pads to make them stand out.

Anime papers

These little square sheets of paper contain intricate patterns and designs, and they look wonderful when decoupaged. There are numerous variations, and they are great for beginners.

Chapter 4

What sort of adhesive is ideal for decoupage?

The following types are the most effective for découpage:

• Découpage glue: This glue is made specifically for this

project and is sold in craft stores. Because it serves as both an adhesive and a varnish, it is perfect.

• PVA glue is an all-purpose adhesive that dries clear and sticks to paper, cardboard, fabric, wood, and metal.

• Permanent spray glue dries rapidly and clearly.

• Gloss varnish is advised since no matter how much coats you apply, it won't become foggy.

What decoupage equipment do I require?

• Scissors: Since cutting out is a major component of the découpage procedure, a pair of tiny, razor-sharp scissors is a need.

• Craft knife: used to cut through intricate regions. Use a craft knife with a razor-sharp edge; otherwise, the paper will rip.

- For precise application of the glue, use a decoupage brush or specialty paintbrush.

- To get rid of the excess adhesive, use a soft sponge or cloth.

- Sandpaper: Use this to smooth down the varnish coats, if necessary.

- Remove any minuscule amounts of excess glue with cotton wool buds.

All of the materials and tools that have been mentioned should be available at your local art and craft shops. These items can all be also purchased online.

Chapter 5

Decoupage: The Basic Technique

- Set up the surface

Once you've decided on the object you want to adorn, make sure the outer layer is immaculate and free of dust considering varnish draws attention to imperfections.

- Reduced images

The images you've chosen should be cut out. It might be less complicated to first rough cut the images out with scissors before precisely cutting them out using a craft knife. If there is still a white border around the cut-out picture, fill it in with a crayon or marker that matches the design or the background it will be placed on.

- Organize the images.

Before you glue the photographs in, make sure you are happy with the positioning. Use tweezers to place tiny photographs.

- Glue the pictures in place

With a slightly damp sponge, smooth out any wrinkles and remove any extra glue.

- Varnish the pictures

Before beginning to varnish, make sure the adhesive is dry. Allow the varnish to completely dry between coats. Depending on how thick the decoupage paper is and how smooth and durable of a finish is wanted, anywhere between four and fifteen coats may be necessary. After a few coats of varnish, you must softly sand the surface and remove all dust to achieve a beautiful lacquered finish. Repeat this procedure until you are satisfied with the result.